D1738061

Your friend

Naomi

Tid-Bits from Africa

True Short Stories

Naomi M. Alldridge

ISBN   9798864144541
Published in the United States of America\
October 24, 2023

Dedication

.   This book is dedicated to Marion Jacobson, for consistently insisting that it should be written.

`   Thank you to the ladies of the Dog Park Coffee Clatch at Sunset Garden Senior Housing, Puyallup, Washington, for censoring and approving each story. It was your encouragement that created the motivation to finish writing these short stories.

        A thank you is extended to my daughter-in-law, Sonya, for so willingly supplying lost photos.

Table of Contents

Preface

I woke up on the airplane somewhere above the central part of Africa. *"I can do this"*, I heard myself thinking. I was so surprised at the lesson I had just taught myself. I am also surprised that it lodged in my memory. I would need that later, but I was unaware of it at that time.

I started my journey in Seattle Washington. The rest of the team was flying from Portland, Oregon. We would meet each other and our missionaries in Johannesburg, South Africa.

That strange statement was the second great surprise of the trip. The first one was when the plane lifted off the ground in Seattle. I had found myself saying *"Thank you Lord for the <u>smooth take-off</u>"*. That was different for me. I had always heard that the take-off and the landing were the most dangerous times of all air flights. I had always prayed very hard during those tense minutes. This time, no prayer, only thanks. I never feared a flight again. I would make that overseas flight alone at least four dozen times in the next thirteen years. My spirit needed both of those reassurances

Two weeks of ministry passed quickly and Sept. 1, 2003, found us on our two airplanes leaving Africa. I had no idea then that one year from that date I would land again on that same airfield. I only felt deep within myself that if my very ill husband should ever be called home to heaven, I would return to that land and help in the Bible College.

Journey with me through the pages of this book. We will walk together through the strange things that can happen to a person when he/she transports him/herself into a culture different from their own. We will share both comical and serious things that I, my family, and friends have experienced within the African setting.

Introduction

Most of these true stories originate in Swaziland, (the country name was changed to Eswatini in 2018) All of these incidents occurred before the name change, so I will use the name Swaziland in this book.

Swaziland, located below the southern 26° latitude, is the smallest country in Africa both in population and land size. The land mass is less than the state of New Jersey. A mountain range lies beside its border to South Africa on the west, and another on the east boarding Mozambique. Between these mountain ranges lie family corrals, large and small plantations, nature reserves, cultural attractions, and many other types of businesses and interesting places.

Within the western range lies the oldest known continually operated iron mine. The ore is transported by truck to Mozambique for smelting. South of this area is Sibebe Rock (see page 20). This granite dome is the largest of its kind in the world and towers over the scenic Pine Valley road. Parallel to the road is a river (see page 10) that tumbles around, between, and over huge boulders. Once you have seen this sight you will not easily forget it.

Painted on the rocks on the eastern range are many pictures attributed to the residents of the Stone Age. These are the pictures you probably saw in your history books when you were a child in school. The ancients made their paints from the red clay present in the soil of the country. One of the oldest skeletons ever found was also in this mountain range.

All names of people in this document have been changed. Unmarried girls are often referred to as Sissi. Unmarried males are called Bobbies. I was usually called Gogo, the SiSwati word for grandmother.

Safari

They sat on the roofless Land Rover, all twelve of those lady tourists. They were unaware of the ways of the wild. Some of them were hatless or sleeveless in the blasting summer sun. Some of them were wearing foot gear that could not protect their feet from the rough thorny ground. All of them were interested in one thing, seeing wild animals.

Their driver-guide told them interesting things as they traveled through the wildlife park. They watched the Hippos lying in the pools of mud, and the Elephants as they limbered slowly down the road. Cameras clicked as they viewed the hedgehogs dashing about, and the Dung Beetles pushing their load of dried feces down a path. Suddenly the driver stopped. There was a White Rhino a short distance from the road.

"You can get out now and take pictures", announced the driver. Twelve ladies sat frozen in the Land Rover. They were speechless with fear. "You can get out and take pictures now", repeated the driver. Finally, one traveler said, "You are serious aren't you"? "Yes" replied their guide. Like an explosion twelve ladies came alive and fairly leaped from the vehicle. Snap, snap, squawked the cameras as the ladies converged on the White Rhino and her baby. "Not too close" warned the driver, and soon he ordered them back into the vehicle. He had just been notified of the location in which a Back Rhino had been spotted. They were usually hard to find.

Black Rhinos and White Rhinos are not so named because of their color. They are all gray. They are named for the shape of their heads and mouths. White, *(it should be wide)*, Rhinos have wide mouths. They cannot lift their heavy heads very far so they eat vegetation on the ground. The Black Rhino, *(it should have been slim)*, has a narrow head and mouth. He can lift his head and eat leaves from the trees. He is said to be the most dangerous of all the wild animals.

The tourists piled back into the Land Rover and the driver headed for a different part of the park. "Now be careful" warned the guide. "This animal will not bother you if you do not get too close. She is lying with her baby some distance from the road. She can get angry if you get too close to that baby". The group headed across the thorny ground. Sure enough, up ahead they saw two humps that looked like two large rocks lying on the ground. Black Rhinoceros.

Cameras clicked as those gals spread out surrounding the big animals. All at once someone got too close. The size of that beast did not slow her down. She sprang to her feet and headed for the invaders of her territory. Twelve ladies and one guard began to run for the road and the safety, they hoped, of the Land Rover. All at once one lady stopped. She had stepped out of her shoe. Although the ground was covered with thorns she turned and went back to retrieve her shoe.

The other eleven adventurers did not stop, they hurried on trying to escape the wrath of the huge angry creature. The tourist retrieved her shoe and turned again to flee from the Black Rhino now bearing down on her. The guide watched helplessly. Suddenly, (he did not know if it would work), he clapped his hands. The Black Rhino stopped, then turned, and walked slowly back to her baby.

Think about that! Would you have gone back for a flip-flop while the most dangerous animal in the world was chasing you?

Black Rhinoceros and her baby, Swaziland

Warthogs—Wild Life Reserve, Swaziland

Giraffe, Wildlife Reserve, Swaziland

What is your status?

I stood in that narrow, hot, hall and waited. I was not alone. Many other people stood silently on the left side of the hall. On the right side were several doors, all shut. Finally, one door opened, and a man rose from the bench that was reserved for the ones at the front of the line. He went into the open doorway, and the rest of us continued to wait. I had all the papers in my hand—passport; police clearance; vaccination records; and my college degree.

Every country has borders and guards to protect its residents, or if they don't, they should. I had been in the country on a visitor's pass, now my 30 days had expired. I had already crossed the border twice to renew it, so, since I wanted to stay in the country, I needed to get a temporary resident permit.

The temperature began to rise in that hallway. We shifted from one foot to the other as we waited. Finally, I reached the bench and had a chance to sit for a little while. The line was still long, then it was my turn to go into the small office.

The officer in charge laid all my documents on her desk and began the questions. Why was I here? What am I doing here? Could a natural citizen do my job? How much am I getting paid for my services? How long do I plan to stay? It seemed she had no end of questions. *'Well, that is good'* I thought. *'Every country needs to be careful of whom they allow to stay within their borders'.*

5

She glanced at the date on one of the documents. "This one is outdated", she announced with disdain. "That is my college degree, the date is the day of graduation", I explained. Obviously embarrassed, she said nothing. The officer shuffled through the rest of the documents.

When finished she copied all the papers, then handed me a sheet of paper. "This document is required for a temporary visa", she announced. "Take this to a doctor then bring it back to me and I will issue you a temporary residence permit for three years".

Yes, they are careful who they allow in. I took the paper and did what she requested. The doctor looked rather annoyed. "Oh, that dumb paper", He grumbled, then signed the document. On my return to the office, I started the waiting process again in that long. narrow. hot hall. Eventually, I was ushered into the small office and received my temporary residence permit.

Oh, so now you want to know what that document referenced? Well, the doctor's signature verified it was true. It was worded something like the following.

"By my authority as a licensed medical physician,
I do proclaim that the following named person,
_____Naomi__Alldridge_____
is not an idiot".

So, what is your status?

The Bridge

The narrow 75-foot or more bridge spans the creek not far from the American Embassy in Ezulwini, Swaziland. It can only accommodate one vehicle at a time, so If you see an approaching car, you simply park and wait  your turn to cross the bridge. The strange thing about this crossing is not the bridge, it is the creek beneath the bridge. If you are standing on the bridge looking upstream the water is clear.

If you are standing on the bridge looking downstream you see that half of the stream is muddy and the other half of the river is running clean. Why? I do not know what has  caused the stream to change in that ten feet beneath the bridge. I am not an Earth Scientist. I am just a reporter.

When I saw this phenomenon I was reminded of James, the earthly brother of Jesus. In his book, he wrote about our instinct to speak ill of others.

> *... no one can tame the tongue. It is an uncontrollable evil filled with deadly poison. With our tongues, we praise our Lord and Father. Yet, with the same tongues we curse people, who were created in God's likeness. Praise and curses come from the same mouth. My brothers and sisters, this should not happen!* *James3: 8-10 GW*

I once knew a lady whose speech could change from sugar-sweet to violent within a second. Her stream was something like the one described above. 'So, what is it', I wonder, 'what happens under our bridges that causes us to slander others'? It causes me to pray, "Lord help me to guard my stream of words so that the water under my bridge runs clean and clear.

Who Has the Right of Way?

It was a hot summer day. I walked slowly down the hill in anticipation of a tall glass of ice-cold lemonade. Bobbie's car was parked under a tree near my home. He had never parked his car there before. What was he doing?

"Hi", I said as I approached the vehicle. "What is going on"? He had a scowl on his face, a bucket beside him, and a rag in his hand. "Hit a cow", he mumbled. Cows can be a real problem in Swaziland. They belong in fenced pastures, but often escape and graze along roads, or enter into open gates. One cow had decided to cross the highway at the wrong moment.

It seems that the brakes on Bobbie's car had failed to respond quickly. The front end of the car had struck the front side of the cow propelling her backward and leveling her rear portions to the exact height of the driver's window. The poor startled cow then lost control of her bowl, spewing its contents through the open window of the car directly into the face of the driver.

Bobbie angrily dipped his rag into the pail and continued his clean-up job. As I stood there picturing the scene I sincerely tried to conceal my laughter. At the time Bobbie did not think it was funny. He continued to clean and gripe. He dipped his rag into the bucket and grumbled as he scrubbed at the mess. By the time he had finished, he despised that car. Better luck next time Bobbie. Maybe you should fix the breaks.

River beside Pine Valley Road, Swaziland

Transportation

Some of us remember leisurely drives through the countryside. That does not happen much anymore. Many of us are on the freeway more and are less often using county roads. Freeways can be hectic. They are crowded with service and goods trucks as well as commuter vehicles. We tend to become tense and nervous. The riders below, on the freeway in Swaziland, do not seem to be upset. They are simply traveling the scenic route. They will probably cackle about their experience.

Traditional Cultural Attire—Cultural Center Swaziland

High School Girls on Cultural Day

High Wire Adventures

What is that? I stopped dead-still on my downhill journey and stared into the sky. Am I really seeing what I think I am seeing?

I grew up in the Pacific Northwestern part of the United States. Squirrels were abundant almost everywhere I had lived. I had often seen them playing in the trees; walking on fences or telephone wires, but not in Africa. In this part of Africa, there seemed to be no squirrels at all. Monkeys, however, were a different story. They abounded on our campus. But monkeys were much larger than squirrels. They could often be seen in trees or on roofs, seldom on fences, but no one ever expected to see them on telephone wires. They were too heavy for that.

The campus of our Bible College is located on a steep hillside. The lowest level houses the living quarters of the staff and students. Directly uphill, approximately the length of one football field is a level containing classrooms, offices, and other buildings. A third level, another football-length uphill, houses the dwelling place of the senior missionary. A telephone wire is stretched high in the sky between the office on the second level and a dwelling on the lower level.

Yes, I did see what I thought I saw. A young monkey stood trembling on that telephone wire. Could he survive up there? He had already come about a third of the distance. He probably would not be able to turn himself around and go back, it was too high to jump down, and he had a long way to go to the destination. I stopped right there to watch.

The youngster was tottering. He wobbled slowly and fearfully placing one foot in front of the other, as the wire swayed. He fought to maintain his balance. Did he look down at the ground in fear? Was he afraid of falling?

I knew exactly how he must be feeling. I remembered my time on the wire. My helmet was on my head. The harness had been fastened around my body and firmly joined to the trolley. My hands gripped the grab-bar, not for my safety, it was just someplace to put my hands. Still, I hesitated. Several people were lined up behind me urging me on. My 79-year-old body stood on that platform viewing the scene below me—far below me. I was scared. This was my last chance to turn back. Encouragement came from behind me, and then I jumped. Off I went down the zip line. I looked at the valley far below. If that wire should give—if my gear should break—if I should fall— that would be immediate death. My heart raced, it was scary, the ground below me was so far down. Then the excitement of the trip took over. Soon I landed safely on the next station, and then the next, and finally, I landed on the eighth and final platform. I was excited, it was a thrill. I had successfully concluded the zip line, but not without fear.

The little monkey was terrified. His small frame shifted in one direction, and then another as he tried to regain stability. He inched forward. Gingerly he tried to maintain control while slowly moving ahead on the unstable wire. Then—he lost his balance.

I looked on the internet for zip-line equipment. I found two types. One for backyard or playground equipment. One for the professionals. The trolley for the backyard lines had a centerpiece attached to the cable, with handles that protruded on both sides of the wire. The security of the rider rested on his ability to grasp the handles and never let go. The tram for professional use was also attached to the wire. This one was joined to a strong harness that firmly held the rider.

I once knew a man who decided to ride one of those homemade zip lines on a hot summer day. He climbed the ladder, wiped the sweat from his hands onto his pants, and firmly grasped the handles of the trolley. He held tightly as he slid gleefully down the wire—and then—his fingers slipped. The hard landing on the ground broke his back. That unfortunate man suffered for the rest of his life.

The little monkey's body tumbled toward the ground so far below. Quicker than you can think his tail swung up and wrapped around the cable. Slowly, he pulled himself back onto the wire and continued his tedious trek. Now—where was my camera when I needed it the most?

In my mind's eye, I still see the monkey on his journey. I see myself on the high wire. Suddenly I wonder, is our life journey somewhat like a zip-line experience? If so, the cable has been stretched tightly from earth to eternity by the Creator. He has placed on that wire a professional gondola that will house us until we reach the destination. One problem—Adam was the first man He placed on that vehicle, and he tampered with it. He made an attachment. He tacked handles onto it. That meant that every person had been launched onto the zipline holding the handles, rather than the gondola housing them.

As we travel down the wire a vast valley appears below us. That is scary. It is especially frightful because the valley below is not a fluffy white cloud, a lush meadow, or even a huge forest. It is a lake—a lake of fire. When one loses his grip on the handles he falls into eternal destruction. However, good news. The trolley has dual controls. When the rider realizes this, he tries to gain entrance into the gondola. He stretches to reach the door, trying as hard as he can but he cannot reach it. If the rider chooses to do so, he can call for help, and immediately God, the maker and operator of the zipline, will reach down and pull him into the gondola. He can relax there and enjoy the ride until his trolley zips safely into the heavenly docking station.

Did the little monkey reach his destination? I do not know. I quit watching and went home.

Coffee Anyone

I am not fond of coffee. I probably would be called a tea drinker. Now, mind you, I will drink a cup of coffee when I am in the presence of others, as it would be a little on the rude side to refuse it. At those times I dump in some sugar and cream and then I can abide it. Now if the crème happens to be flavored with something like caramel or hazelnut, I might enjoy it a little bit. Acholic beverages? No, the strongest I can take is Root Beer or Pepsi.

My friends, Art and Betty Littlefield, retired pastors, were also volunteers at the Bible College where I volunteered. They often took me with them when going out somewhere. There were not many restaurants in the small village, or surrounding communities, where we lived in Africa. Oh, yes, there was the Chinese place, and the Portuguese place next to it in the mall, but the nice one was in the new Hotel across the street from the mall. That one we enjoyed.

One beautiful summer afternoon we settled ourselves on the veranda at the hotel. The waitress promptly approached and asked for our drink preference. Art quickly ordered coffee, and then Betty ordered coffee. I sat there a moment, then asked, What flavors of coffee do you have"? She rapidly started down the list. It was long, and she was talking fast. Finally, I said, "That one. By that time she had gone on to the next one. "Irish coffee"? she asked. Confused I thought, *'That is not what I intended to order— but—Irish--and the image of four-leaf clovers filled my mind, then Mint—isn't mint Irish too I reasoned. Irish coffee must be mint flavored'.* "Yes, that will be fine".

We sat there on the veranda of the courtyard, enjoying the glint of the sun on the nearby swimming pool. Our waitress brought our coffee and I dumped in the required cream and sugar. Betty quietly suggested, "Isn't Irish coffee made with alcohol"? No, I answered, it must be mint", and I took a sip of coffee. Funny, it did not taste a bit like mint, and I could not smell mint either. Dinner arrived and it was delicious. I took another sip of coffee. I did not like the stuff at all. "I think they use whisky to make Irish coffee", Betty inserted into the conversation. "Think so"? I asked. I took a few more skimpy sips throughout dinner, then left most of the coffee in the cup at the end of the meal. Was she right?

Back home again I opened the computer. "What are the ingredients of Irish coffee"? I asked Google. The answer? Coffee and whisky. Oops. No wonder I did not like that mint flavoring—it was not mint!

Parade

Bong, Bong, Bong, Bong! The loud sound rebounded through my open window. The drumming sounded almost like a parade. A parade? No, not way out here. I peeked out the window. Yes, there was a parade. A monkey parade. (see page 52) The starting point was the high bank near the rear of the men's dormitory. One by one they came, leaping across the six-foot distance from the bank to the roof of the structure that sat below and to the north of me.

Most of these monkeys were mothers. They clasped their babies to their chests, made the leap, then detached the little ones and began the instruction of the art of drumming. Bong, rang out the sound of their feet striking the tin roof as they raced down the length of the building They hopped down onto and crossed the front porch roof. Each mother stopped, retrieved her offspring, swirled her body 180 degrees as she jumped off the porch, grabbed the slick steel pipe that supported the roof, and slid like a fireman to the ground.

Suddenly one monkey, halfway down the pole. stopped sliding. Then she climbed back up that steel pole, sprang onto the roof above her, snatched up a young monkey, slapped him to her chest, and slid back down the pole. She had forgotten her baby. I laughed as I remembered an event that happened years before.

We were in church. My baby was asleep in the nursery, and my other children sat beside me on the bench.

The service ended, and everyone exited the building. I ushered the children to the car while my husband turned out the lights and locked the edifice. He got in the car and we started home. When we were almost there someone said, "Where is the baby"? We turned around and went back to the church. He was still sound asleep in the nursery. All of us had forgotten our baby. I knew just how that monkey felt.

That was the only monkey I ever saw climb up the pole. Now, how did she manage to climb that slippery steel pole?

Sibebe Rock, Swaziland

Power of a Seed

We do not normally think of a seed as powerful. They are little. We can hold hundreds of small seeds in the palm of our hand. Yet, many of them hold a power far greater than we do.

I was astonished the first time I saw one. A small seed had lodged in a crevice in the rook, sprouted, grown, and its roots, then its trunk, had divided the rock. Its branches and leaves towered above the split rock. I saw many of these in Swaziland. No doubt they are in other places as well.

Swaziland

The seed in the rock above did not stop growing with germination. Although the tree in the picture above is not there now it did continue to grow until it became large. The rock gave way to the tree.

The rock in the picture below sits beside the home of one of my friends. Generations of children have played tag in and around its base. The tree in the picture below is no longer there either. It became huge, dividing the rock halves farther and farther apart. Then the tree died and rotted away. This rock is more than twice my height The halves are now about two feet apart.

Is it possible to walk through a rock? Of course not. Yet that small, insignificant seed made it possible. I have walked through this huge rock Many people look at the impossible and give up. With God all things are possible.

Near Tea Road, Swaziland

If He can create a seed and give it the ability to do the impossible, could He also grant unto humans that He has created, the ability to do the impossible also? One day Jesus was talking to his disciples and He told them *"...If you can believe, all things are possible to him who believes"*. *(Mark 9:23)*

We Are Going to be Engaged

I was surprised when I met them at the mini-mall. I was unaware of any romantic attraction between the two, but the gleam in their eyes told the story. "Hi", I greeted them. "What are you two doing down here?" After an awkward pause, Sissi suggested to the young man that they tell me. It was still a secret. "Gogo, we are going to be engaged".

Now that sounds strange to the ears of a person from the West, but not to them. I had heard the expression before. Marriages must be arranged and the bride purchased by the groom. It meant there would be a two-family meeting. First, the families would decide if the wedding would take place, and then negotiate the bride price. That could be anywhere up to 15 or 20 cows. If the bride were the youngest girl in the family the price would be higher as she was the last girl to work for her father. If her last name happened to be the same as the last name of the king, the price would be many cows or the equivalent of them in money. After the bartering ended there would be an announcement of the engagement. That would be at a ceremony conducted with a party. One or two of the cows would be killed, and a barbeque held for friends and family.

Occasionally the groom may not be able to obtain enough cows before the wedding ceremony. When this happened, he could pay the bill to his father-in-law when he was able to do so. However, should the new family have a baby daughter, she became the property of the bride's father until the bill was paid. If that daughter should grow up and marry, with the bill unpaid, the bride price would go to the grandfather, or if he was not living an uncle may claim the bride price. Daughters were valuable.

When each male child was still quite small, his father would give him a cow. His goal would be to multiply his herd during his youth to the size required for the bride price.

Sissi bore the sir name of the king. I once heard her say, "The bride price for me will be 20 cows, and I am worth it!" I do not know the final bride price this groom paid. I left the country before the wedding, but they did get married.

Rural Driving School, Swaziland

24

You Just Never know

In Swaziland, the measurement of time means very little, especially in rural areas. For example, a ceremonial event may be announced to begin at a certain time, but guests will begin to arrive much later. That explains my confusion the first time I heard the time of an event announced 5 o'clock for 7. For a scheduled event of another type, people may arrive closer to the announced time. This day was definitely the former.

I was waiting for graduation to begin. I was at a church in Manzini where I had been teaching one night a week. True to Swazi culture they were running about two hours late in beginning the ceremony. No surprise— everyone must have known it would be that way as very few people were waiting for the service to begin, including graduates, who had not yet arrived. The sun beat upon us mercilessly, so I seated myself on a bench in the shade. Slowly others came and sat beside me.

I did not remember ever being in that church before the Sunday I had preached for them a few months earlier. As I waited a young man approached me. He greeted me by name which surprised me as I do not recall ever meeting him. I had not. He said "I have been waiting eight years to meet you. You preached in this church eight years ago and I gave my life to the Lord. I have not told anyone this, as I wanted to tell you first, and this is the first time I have seen you".

I was stunned. It must not have been me. It must have been someone else. I did not preach anywhere eight years ago. I was still in denial that God wanted me to preach. "Yes", the young man said. "It was you who preached that day. Thank you".

I thought back. Eight years ago? At that time Arthur Littlefield often preached in churches around the area. I usually went with him and Betty to the services. It was understood that whenever you visited a church, especially a rural church, you would say a few words of greeting. Had that happened?

I looked at the building again. In my mind, I remembered a building similar to this, where the seating in the sanctuary was placed in the other direction. The outside was different too. Was it possible? Had Arthur preached here? Had they remodeled this place? Yes, undoubtedly, I had given a testimony in this building that had touched this young man's life. I feel greatly humbled. You just never know!

I Want to be Adopted

Bobbie paced back and forth across my kitchen. On each trip, he paused a moment to look at the Banana Cream Pie that sat on the counter. The meringue tips had been baked to a perfect golden-brown color. The second-year students had gathered at my home for dinner, and it was not quite ready.

Bobbie could not take his eyes off that pie. He had never seen one before. You could never find a pie like that in the local supermarkets or bakeries. Pies here were more like what Westerners would call large tarts.

"Gogo made that pie" commented his female classmate Sissi. "No, she didn't" replied Bobbie. "Yes, she did" affirmed Sissi. "No, she could not have made it" declared Bobbie. "Oh yes, she did" Sissi insisted.

With that, Bobbie turned to me. "Did you make that pie?" he asked. I told him I had made that pie. "Oh," he said thoughtfully, then brightened and said, "I want to be adopted".

Tree beside the Indian Ocean in Mozambique
It has now fallen into the ocean

Twins

Pastor Mikel Jacobson, missionary and local pastor, stood beside the casket. You would expect him to know what to say, but even a pastor has times when his words do not come easily. In the casket lay a teenage girl. Her twin sister stood in tears at the edge of the open grave.

There is a special bond between twins that other family members do not enjoy. They have been together since conception. Their lives have been shared like no others. Their daily activities have been learned together. It appears they sometimes even share the same thoughts. Now one had experienced death alone and the other must learn to live alone.

Beside the weeping girl stood her brother. It appeared he was there to comfort his sister. Around them were other family members and friends. Pastor Jacobson said the final words, "Ashes to ashes—dust to dust—into God's hands we commit her spirit". The pallbearers moved to lower the casket into the gaping hole in the ground. Quickly the brother pushed his sister into the open grave just as the casket was about to be lowered.

"STOP", cried the pastor. "Take her out of there". The pallbearers stood back. "No, they were born together. They must die together", exclaimed the brother. "It is not normal for two babies to be born together, therefore, they must also die together". "Take her out of there" ordered the pastor again. Someone did.

It is not unusual for this sentiment to be found in many places in Africa. A normal birth is usually one baby. Two babies at once are so unlucky that one, or both are sometimes left to die. Western thought is different. People in the West consider multiple births to be a double blessing. This family considered twins to have brought bad luck to the family. One was now gone, the other should follow.

The pastor arranged for the living twin to be taken to a place of safety. There she was cared for until she had recovered from the trauma. As of this writing, she is still there, busily helping others in their time of need.

Yesterday-Today-Tomorrow Plant, Swaziland.
On the first day, the flower is purple,
On the second day, it is lavender,
On the third day, it is white,
the next day it is shriveled and dead.

Lucky

"Lucky", Sharon called from her place beside the corner of the fenced pasture. My visiting sister, camera in hand, backed away from the fence. Out there somewhere in the pasture, a huge animal raised his head. He knew that voice. It belonged to the one who had cradled him while feeding him his bottles when he was a baby. Like a favorite puppy, he had spent the first six months of his life sleeping on the foot of her bed. He was named Lucky because his mother had died the day he was born and everyone considered him lucky to be alive. The second six months of his life he had slept on the foot of the bed of one of the employees. By the time Lucky was a year old he had grown so large that he had been placed in a pasture.

Sharon's late husband had been the manager of a large sugar plantation in southern Swaziland. Together with their talented employees, they built this Wild Life Reserve. After her husband's decease, Sharon moved away and the efficient employees ran the Reserve by themselves.

"Lucky", Sharon called again. "Lucky", echoed John, the employee who daily cared for the animal. Out of the middle of the pasture bounded a lion. The big brute was at least six feet in length not including his tail. A huge main hung around his head and shoulders. He ran eagerly to the fence like a puppy anxious to greet his master. Sharon spoke lovingly to him and rubbed his main.

"You can pet him now", she told me. She was standing near his head, John was next to her, and I was closer to the lion's rear section. Both Sharon and John were stroking his back and talking to him. Gingerly I reached through the wire fence and stroked the lion on his back. A thrill shot through me. I was petting a lion! A huge lion! My sister stood frozen in place. My hands worked their way up his back. This was amazing. I stroked closer and closer to his head. Suddenly Sharon noticed me. Not so close, she warned. Stay away from his head, after all, he may be tame but he is a wild animal. I restricted my petting to Lucky's back. After a while, we said goodbye to Lucky and left the Reserve.

The lion sadly watched us leave, then turned, and wandered into the pasture from wherever he had come. So—what happened to Lucky? I have been told that eventually, Lucky became so large that he was removed from the Reserve and placed in a zoo.

Did my sister get a good picture? Well, I assume she did. I really do not know. I never saw a copy of that picture.

Where is the Coin?

The old termite-riddled building was sided with a single layer of slab[1]. A wide crack between the boards allowed for some appreciated ventilation during the summer months and furnished reasons for shivering in the winter months. A tin roof covered the ceiling-less structure which magnified the soft sound of raindrops to one of thunderous proportions during the rainy season. A nail hole in the roof allowed the sun to shine through producing a round yellow circle of light on the hard-packed dirt floor.

Today the small church was packed with over 200 happy people seated on the backless benches, then standing, dancing, and singing joyfully in worship. A very small boy danced up and down the aisle, exactly mimicking his elders in dance movements. The toddler was nearly a professional already.

When the sermon concluded the pastor began his usual announcements, then launched into a lengthy detail of current business for his congregation. The toddler, tired of sitting still, wandered down the aisle. Suddenly he noticed the circle on the floor. It looked exactly like a gold coin lying on the dirt floor, so he bent down to pick it up. His shadow blocked out the light—no coin on the floor.

Puzzled, the little boy stood up, and behold the coin was visible. Again, he bent down to pick it up, and again, it suddenly disappeared. What happened to his coin? The

---

[1] A slab is the unsalable first board cut from a log at the sawmill. It has the curve of the tree on one side and is flat on the other side.

child straightened, and behold the coin appeared. He bent again, and the coin was gone. Highly confused the boy stood up and shifted his position.

Suddenly the coin appeared on the floor. This time when the toddler bent down his shadow did not cover the object, so his little fingers curved to pick up the edge of the coin, and nothing was there. Now he was more confused than before. He tried, time after time to find the edge of the coin, delighting me and the children on a nearby bench.

Soon a young girl came from the rear of the building and capturing the child returned him to his mother. I wonder, will he look for the coin next week?

Rutul Church in Swaziland

The Village

Swaziland's million-plus people live in an area a little smaller than the state of New Jersey. Seventy-five percent of them live on small family plots in the rural portion of the country. Eighty-five percent of the poverty-stricken residents are those in rural areas. When any type of disaster occurs, these are the people who it affects the most.

A modern four-lane freeway stretches across Swaziland. Many paved two-lane roads span the kingdom. From these highways, mud roads zig-zag through the entire country leading to tiny villages and family farm plots. One tiny village lies deep in the heartland of Swaziland. It is located beside a high-banked river. If you drive down that red-dirt road you will find many unique family farms dotting the countryside.

This area of Swaziland had a severe problem. It had not rained for three years, and the impoverished people relied solely on the rain for watering their crops. The draught was bringing severe hardship to all of Swaziland. It had created a food shortage and the cattle were dying. Although water flowed in the nearby river, the native people groups had no way to move the water from the river canyon to the hard-crusty land except by hand-hauled bucket, and that was not enough for crops. The natives had done everything they knew to solve the problem. They had done the rain dances. They had prayed to the gods. They had used every fetish and potent they had ever heard of, but still no rain.

Within the International Church in Ezulwini, there was a group of good-hearted people who cared for others in need. They had long been known to feed and clothe the elderly and orphans. They learned about the problem in this village. One young man I shall call Paul, and two of his friends decided to help the people in that tiny village. They purchased a generator and a pump and went to visit the village.

Local chiefs control all rural areas, so the trio went to see the chief. He gathered his people and they discussed the matter. They seemed skeptical of the option. It appears that they had not seen a generator and pump in operation and doubted it could help them. The three had also asked for permission to build a church for the village. That request was violently opposed and brought a final NO to the project. The trio went back to their car and started the engine. Where no help was wanted, no help could be given.

Then the chief thought, 'What if? He ran to the car, and said, "Wait, let's talk". Paul rolled down the window. "God just now told me something", he announced to the chief. "He wants you to know that He loves you. To prove that He loves you He is going to send you rain in twenty minutes". That looked impossible to Paul, his friends, and the chief. It had not rained one drop in three years. There were no storm clouds in the sky. The chief and his people laughed. That was a bunch of nonsense. He turned away from the car.

But Paul knew he had heard God speak. He turned off the engine, and with his friends, sat there. The minutes dragged by. No wind. No storm clouds. Hot, just like yesterday. The villagers stood around with total disdain for the visitors. Nineteen minutes went by. No rain. The seconds counted down. Twenty minutes! A few drops of water fell from the sky—then more—then a storm hit that community. The residents of that village danced around in glee. The friends in the car rejoiced and thanked God.

A church was built in that village. One of its young men went to Bible School and became their pastor. That little village prospered from the water pumped from the river, and from God, whom they learned to love and serve.

Did God love them? Does God love us? Yes, God does love all of us, and He does care for us too!

Sunday School Class at Rural Church in Swaziland

Execution Mountain in Swaziland, used until the late 1960's

Hikers placing memorial stones
on the trail up Execution Mountain

Mulenga Kapwepwe

The Bantu people are made up of many tribes throughout Africa. In ancient times they migrated west across the northern part of Africa to the Atlantic Ocean. Later migrations took them down the west coast to the central part of the continent and then east across central Africa to the Indian Ocean. Still, later migrations took them south to the southern tip of Africa. The last migration was when the Swazis, who separated from their Zulu cousins, came north. They settled in and married with, the peace-loving people who lived in the land. The area became known as Swaziland. Through the centuries of migration, the Bantu people left tribes at many places along the way. This explains the similarity of customs and traditions throughout Africa.

There is a large group of Bantu people in Zambia. One of the traditions of the Bantu in Zambia is a ceremony called the Mulenga Kapwepwe. It is basically a food and service festival welcoming the groom into the family and traditions of the bridal family. Family and friends of both families are there but the bride is not allowed to attend the festive occasion, it is prepared especially for the groom.

One of my female students from Zambia found a soulmate in Swaziland. She took him home to Zambia for the wedding ceremony. I was visiting Zambia and was invited to the Mulenga Kapwepwe party

Long before party time, the drums began to sound. Women gathered outdoors preparing food on outdoor fires.

Children ran around playing games. I was ushered, along with others, into the living room. There we waited. The groom was seated in a chair of honor. We talked. When all was ready the party began.

Drums beat out a tune instigating the beginning of the festival. The ladies who had been cooking formed a parade. They carried on their heads, pots of food wrapped in all-purpose cloths. The leader, assuming the role of the bride, advanced into the room carrying a basin of water and a towel. She knelt and bowed before the groom, and then removed his shoes. She bathed and dried his feet all the while assuring him of her continued lifelong practice of serving him and making him comfortable. After kissing his feet, she arose and went into another part of the house.

One by one the ladies entered. Each one removed the bundle from her head and placed it at the feet of the groom. She bowed low, removed the pot from its cloth container, and showed and explained to him the food she had brought. Then she arose and placed the pot on a buffet table.

The lady who represented the bride reappeared and placed a cup of Kava brew in the hand of one of the guests. Kava brew is a liquor made from the fruit of the Kava tree. In this ceremony, orange soda was substituted for the brew. Each visitor, as well as the groom, took a sip from the communal cup. Drinking this cup was a covenant to support this new family unit.

Soon a plate loaded with food was brought to me. There on the plate was a large portion of something. I had seen these black ones before. Another student had guided me through the marketplace of his village. He had pointed them out to me as something pregnant women ate for good luck with their babies. No one was pregnant here. They must be for good luck with marriages also.

Could I eat them? I pushed them around on the plate. To leave them would be disrespectful. Finally, I opened my mount, shoved one in, and swallowed. Not too bad. Ok, I will try another. I placed another one in my mouth. The small hairs ticked my throat. That would have to be enough!

Late that night my host drove me to the place where I was staying. Did you eat any of the caterpillars", he asked. I could truthfully say that I did. "Oh, aren't they good" he replied. "They are a real delicacy". Well, maybe they are good, I do not know. I swallowed them whole.

Elephants in Wildlife Reserve, Swaziland

Example of Rural Fenced Cattle Corral
Cultural Center in Swaziland

Exotic House on Tea Road--Swaziland

Hungry Anyone?

I had not been in Swaziland long when I was invited to an Ethiopian dinner party. My Ethiopian student took me to Manzini. There we met about five Ethiopian doctors and their families. A member of one of the families was leaving Swaziland, thus the farewell dinner. Ethiopian food is rich in spices. Often the curry sauce has whole hard-boiled eggs in it, and it is served over rice. The meal is served with bread that looks like a thin sheet of Styrofoam. I was told that one of the qualities a young man looks for when thinking of marriage is the young lady's ability to make good bread. The diner tears off a piece of bread and uses it to scoop up his food. No spoons or forks thank you! They kindly furnished me with a fork. I did try eating the Ethiopian way at a later dinner. I was so sloppy that the hostess soon draped a large tablecloth over my clothing. I guess they were not too impressed with my table manners.

Ethiopian coffee is different and interesting. A young lady brought a small pot with a long spout to the center of the courtyard. She sat down on the ground and ground the coffee beans in a small grinder, put the ground coffee in the pot, and filled it with water. Over a small heating device, she brought the coffee to a boil and boiled it for some time. The very thick brew was served in small cups with plenty of sugar.

Swaziland sauce that is served over rice or pop is much thinner than the Ethiopian version. It has a little meat and vegetable content but is more soup-like. Oh, what is pop? Well, not a soft drink! It is made from ground white corn. When cooking, the meal is poured slowly into boiling water and briskly beaten. When finished it is thick and looks like mashed potatoes. Taste? Well, not at all like mashed potatoes. It reminds me a little bit of Grits which is so loved in the southern part of the US. Although I am not fond of Grits, I prefer them to Pop.

What do you think? I think I would much rather just have mashed potatoes.

And then there is Zambia, but—you already know about the delicacy called caterpillars.

Very Nice Rural Family Corral

Bobbie
(A Journal Entry—(September 2016)

Bobbie entered my Math classroom when one-fourth of the semester was over. I could tell right away that he had trouble understanding me. That is not strange, as Swazis learned British English, and American English is difficult at first for them to understand. I told them to ask me to slow down or to repeat so they would understand, but like most Swazis, he in kindness, said nothing about it and continued in ignorance of whatever I was saying. To make things worse he seemed a little slow in understanding the principles of mathematics, probably because of his late entrance into the class. All those three things made his introduction to college difficult. Bobbie is a very likable kid. A huge smile, bright even teeth, and a pleasant personality make this student very welcome in and out of the classroom

With only two new first-year students no beginning class for computers was open for them, so they entered the other classes. The other new student was already familiar with computer technology. That left Bobbie the only one in school who knew nothing about the machine, and thereby completely unable to type the required projects for each class—so I started a special tutoring class in the afternoon just for him.

A first-year student is never asked to preach in chapel, that just is not done. However, I walked into chapel one morning and Bobbie was the speaker of the day. I was surprised to see that he was already preaching very well.

This afternoon three male students and I were in the library. At first, I thought they were teasing Bobbie, for they are notorious teasers, but then I realized what they were saying was really deep admiration for the young man. In the middle of the conversation, he told me he wanted to give me his testimony.

A few weeks ago, on a Friday at the close of my class, I had asked all who were preaching that weekend to come to the middle of the room. The rest of us gathered around them and prayed God's blessing on them as they ministered. He was one of those students who had come forward. He thanked me for being anointed by God to do that. Was I anointed? I do not know. It was something I had done before at times and suddenly decided to do again that day. He had gone to a funeral that evening and ended up preaching with an anointing that night and again the next day. After the other two men left he opened up and talked more with me about his life.

He was the middle child of seven children. All of the others were healthy but he was a very sick child, often at the point of death. His parents took him to doctors, to hospitals, to the traditional healers *(witch doctors),* but nothing seemed to help. His life was a series of <u>mooti</u>, *(traditional witch-craft methods of herbs, portents, and fetishes).* Finally, his parents gave up on him and said that the gods could just have him if they wanted him.

I do not know at what age in his childhood, or how it happened, but somewhere he learned of Jesus, accepted

46

Him as Saviour, and was healed of all his diseases. His older three siblings had been sent to school until they could read and write their names, then put to work. He did not have that privilege. When his father realized he was well, he sent him off to be a cattle herder and earn money for the family.

At about 13 or 14 years of age, he came home one day and asked to go to school. He wanted to read the Bible for himself, not just listen to what others told him. His father was adamant that he return immediately to herd the cattle. After words with his father Bobbie ran away from home. He was eventually befriended by someone, taken in, clothed, fed, and sent to school. He was 14 when he entered first grade and began preaching at about that time. He did well in school and was appreciated by the headman because he advised the children to obey and not to fight. He graduated from High School, the only one in his family to do so.

Bobbie found his way into hospitals. He has a soft heart for the sick and communicates well with them as he knows how they feel. He is currently a hospital chaplain, unpaid, but is given gifts as God directs others to give to him. As he leaves the campus today, he will attend a funeral where he will be preaching. Tomorrow and Sunday he will spend most of the day in the hospital. He will preach early in the morning. Then he will be with the staff, then go from patient to patient in the hospital, and finally, preach again in the courtyard in the early afternoon.

Bobbie was surprised when I told him my late husband spent the last nine years of his ministry as a hospital chaplain. He seemed not to realize that the profession he was in was one already in existence. He just feels that God has called him to work with the sick and afflicted so he does. It seems the police and hospital personnel in his area of Swaziland recognize the passion he possesses and call for him. He thinks the Devil has tried to destroy him, but God healed him and gave him a job to do.

I pray for a life of blessing for Bobbie as he continues in God's service.

The Author with Swaziland Lady and Her Baby

48

Frogs
(A journal Entry)

This morning I went out back to water my avocado plants. I have two of them, seedlings, in pots under my bedroom window. I watered them yesterday and left a half-full pail of water beside them. In this hot weather, the ground drinks up water incredibly fast. Swimming happily in that pail was a frog. I had never seen one like him out here. He looked much like a toad I would have met in the US. Well, I watered my plants and sent the unhappy frog on his way elsewhere.

I had grown up believing that all frogs are green. Well—I knew of the brown variety, but we called them toads, not frogs. Once, long ago, when I was cultivating my flower bed with a small hand rake, I noticed a large clump of soil. I picked it up. Not soil! The dirt mass was soft. I quickly released that toad.

Did you know there are poison frogs? I was not aware of that until one of my students, who was very much afraid of frogs, pointed that out to me. I had a hole in my front yard that turned out to be the entrance to the home of a family of frogs. My foot had slipped into that hole and I almost fell so I was going to fill up that hole so I would not fall. Before I got that done, I saw frogs coming and going from the hole. I was not going to stop up the door to their home. When my student found that out he filled up the hole quickly. He was so afraid of poisonous frogs that he regarded all frogs as dangerous, therefore all frogs must be avoided. He told me the poisonous ones are red. I searched on the internet and found many kinds of colorful frogs, some were not poisonous, and many were. Green frogs, and toads, are all I had ever seen. I felt so bad about closing the door to the frog's home that a few days later I opened it up again.

One very warm day I wandered over the bridge to have a backyard picnic and watch the children play in the swimming pool. There, around the pool in the early evening, were hundreds of frogs. They were about one inch in length. As they opened their mouths the pouch beneath them began to swell to more than twice the size of their bodies. As they released their very loud crooks the swelling reduced and the frogs were of normal size again.

One day I was in the bathroom when I suddenly noticed something in the doorway hopping across the floor. A frog! A red frog! Was he poison? How was I going to get out of the bathroom? How was I going to get that frog out of the house? Question after question ran through my mind as I sat there watching that thing hop, and I asked the Lord those questions too! Finally, I got up, grabbed a towel, and tossed it over the frog. Then I scooped him up, walked calmly to the back door, and shook the towel depositing him outside. Where did he go? I do not know, and I did not care, as long as he did not re-enter that door.

That reminds me of a nice healthy green frog that I met some time ago. I was going to South Africa with some friends. We always stopped at the South African border restroom when we traveled that road rather than the Swaziland border restroom. It was much more inviting to our Western standards. When I rose from the toilet that day and started to flush it, I found to my surprise a frog in the bowl. "Well, hello," I said to him. Then I said "goodbye" and flushed him down the toilet.

So, what will be my next frog encounter?

Elephants on Wild Life Reserve in Swaziland

51

Monkeys on the Roof—Story page 19

Impala, in the Hlane Royal National Park, Swaziland

Pot-Holes

I was unprepared for the spectacular scene. Sure, I had heard the term *Pot potholes*, but to me, it just meant holes in a paved road. No one ever explained the phenomena to me.

I was with Judith. We had just been on safari in Kruger Park, South Africa. We had already enjoyed watching the wild animals. We had already visited several beautiful waterfalls and gone through famous caves. Now we were standing above the potholes. What a scene! I did not expect this. Judith and I started down the steep path to observe the potholes at closer range. The streams had long since washed downriver all of the soil leaving a huge gorge with solid rock sides and bottom. We crossed bridges that spanned the rivers, then we set foot on rocks near some of the smaller pot-holes where the river had changed its course. What are they? Glad you asked.

The bed of both rivers is solid rock. One might say it is the soul of the river. Potholes are circular holes cut into the rocks at the spot where two rivers come together. One river flows lazily through the countryside. A second river comes rushing angrily down the mountain into the face of the s sluggish current. The force of the faster current causes it to swirl to the right creating a downward whirling circle, much like a whirlwind creates an upward circle. Over time the swirling water cuts into the rock creating a deep circular hole. There were many pot-holes at this location, some small, others large and deep. This forever changed the nature of the river. Spectacular.

Gorge created by the Pot-Holes

I wonder. Is the life of a human a little bit like the life of a river? Each tiny spring flows downward, connecting with other springs and creeks and rivers until it flows into the sea. From birth to death each human life interacts with hundreds of other people.

I find myself questioning, "What kind of a stream am I? Am I a lethargic creek that can be affected by other angry turbulent personalities; or am I a forceful river that interacts with vengeance on the lives of others? Or am I strong enough, yet mild enough to make an impression on other streams while maintaining my own identity? A river cannot predict its course, but humans can determine their destiny! It causes me to think, and to pray, "God, with your help I will maintain a current that will not permit the turbulence of others to drill holes into my soul".

So, are pot-holes spectacular? Yes, they are, in the life of a river. In humans? No, they are not.

Smaller holes in sections of the former location
of the riverbed

Above- Safari Housing In South Africa —Below-Swaziland

Help!

It was big! It was on my window—no, it was inside my window—on the inside of my translucent window curtain. Its body must be almost as big as my fist, and its thick black legs extend another body length. It would not have bothered me if it were only ¾ of an inch long like the ones I was familiar with, but this thing was a handbreadth in width This was no ordinary spider. I shivered in dread as I looked at the silhouette of the huge thing. How would I get rid of it?

I had seen one a few ago on my kitchen ceiling. One passing Bobbie came in and got rid of it for me—but he was not around anymore, what could I do this time? I definitely would not go near that thing!

I looked at the silhouette again—from a distance. Then, through the window, I noticed a young man walking up the path, talking on his cell phone. I quickly called to him. Bobbie came in, still talking on the phone.

I pointed to the spider inside my curtain. Bobbie shifted his phone slightly, and mouthed, "You want me to get it down?" "Yes", I nearly screamed.

Bobbie shook the curtain and swatted the spider, who came tumbling to the floor. Bobbie never missed a word of conversation on his phone. I looked at him in terror. "You want me to kill it"? Bobbie mouthed again. "Yes", I almost shouted.

Bobbie stepped on the spider, then exited through the door and calmly continued his uphill journey, never missing a word of his phone conversation. Me? I trembled for a while, swept the thing off the floor with a paper towel, and mopped the floor. Then I thanked God there were some Bobbies around.

Lion Park near Johannesburg, South Africa

Anybody Home?

There are times when you may be lonely and wish someone would come to visit you. There are also times when you would rather, they would not visit you. Sometimes it is surprising to see who has come to visit you.

Art and Betty Littlefield drove slowly up their long driveway. They parked the car and sat there in disbelief. There, right there at their front door. Visitors? Not anyone they were expecting.

The big one was standing on his hind legs. Another big one was standing on his hind legs too—on the shoulders of the first monkey. He reached upward—he stretched as far as possible. Then he pulled the chain and rang the doorbell over and over again. Anybody home?

Monkey on my bedroom window sill

59

Hippos wallowing in the med—Royal Nature Park—Swaziland

Zoo in Johannesburg, South Africa

Confused Directions

At first, I thought it was just me. I could not figure out directions. North seemed to be south, and south seemed to be north. I knew exactly where the sun came up and went down, but still, during the mid-day, east seemed to be west, and west seemed to be east. Maybe this was because I was now in the Southern Hemisphere, instead of my lifelong time in the Northern Hemisphere. I thought that after a while I would get used to this, but I did not. Then I learned that most of the other missionaries were having the same problem. It was not just me.

Many of our students were already pastors before coming to school. Some others found a place where there was no church and started one, usually, this was in a school building. Bobbie was one of those students. He found a place in the country that had a school, started a church, and had about 50 or more people attending his services. This place was accessed by a paved road for about an hour's drive, and then another half hour over a very rough dirt road that was impassable during heavy rains. He usually rode out there on a Combi *(public transport vehicle),* sometime Saturday and stayed the night with someone from the church.

One weekend my visiting son Andrew, and daughter-in-law, Shirley, and I decided to drive him out Sunday morning and visit his church. We loaded into the Rav4, men in the front seat, Shirley and I in the back seat. We enjoyed the ride out and the lively meeting with his people, even though we did not understand anything said during the service. Services are usually held in the native language of SiSwati; because orphans and the elderly seldom speak English.

After the service, Bobbie asked us to drive by his family home. He needed something but also wanted to introduce us to his mother. He knew a shortcut road to get there. We went on another back-country road I had never been on before. It was in a desolate mountain countryside. The road was continually going up and down steep hills and around curves. Eventually, Shirley and I began talking about directions. We had no idea where we were, or which direction was which. Finally, I said. "Bobbie, what direction are we traveling"? "Down", came the immediate answer.

We all burst into laughter. I learned something that day. There are lots of directions, not just four. Along with north; south; east and west there are also up and down, and over there.

Balanced

Talk about the unusual! I have seen mountains with meadows, bare mountains, forested mountains, and some rocky mountains, but never a mountain that looked like these. My son, Richard, and I had just traveled up a mountain so steep we felt like we had taken off in a jet plane. Near the top of the mountain, we found a signless road. My son happens to be a very curious person, so we drove down that road. The road soon became narrow, then a path, then not much more than a trail. There was no place to turn around so we kept on going.

We crossed a broken-down plank bridge, then the trail opened again. Before long we found ourselves on a narrow road at the base of a rocky hill. The crest of the hill was lined with huge odd-shaped boulders. Many stones were balanced on top of other large boulders. Sometimes the lower rock was somewhat smooth at the top. Sometimes the crest of the lower rock was a peak of its own. Can you imagine a basketball balanced on a spool of thread? That is the best way I can describe those rocks. We marveled at them!

How were these created? Technology would never have done this way back in a place where few people have been. In fact, it could not have been done anywhere. These things must have been here for thousands of years. How did they stand the hurricane winds of the area or the earthquakes that frequently occurred here? They must have been here since the dawn of creation, and the creator himself must have designed and maintained them.

We drove around the bend of the mountain. There, in the shadow of a huge balanced boulder sat a house. It was not new. It had probably housed several generations of children. I thought '*Would I have the trust to live in that house'?* God had kept it safe all those years, yet, would I trust enough to live there? *Would you?*

Smaller Balanced Rock on Pine Valley Road, Swaziland

Charlie

I do not think he has a name—well, maybe in monkey language he does, but I do not speak that language. Usually, we just call him one of those monkeys. I will call him Charlie. He often comes down the hill and watches the man with the big black car. I sometimes wonder what he thinks. Perhaps it is something like this.

'Here comes the man in the big black car. I like the big black car. I like the man. The man gets in the car and, puts his hands on that big round thing and looks out the window, and the big black car takes him somewhere. Then, soon, it brings him back again. I would like to have a big black car. Oh look, the man is getting out of the big black car. He is going away. Now I can look closely at the big black car'.

Charlie approaches the big black car. He looks at the front. He touches the back, then he walks around to the other side. The man forgot something. The window is open. Quickly Charlie jumps through the open window. He hops into the backseat. He looks out the back window. He feels inside the pocket on the door, then the pocket on the back of the front seat. Nothing is in them. No food there. Charlie jumps back into the front passenger seat. He sees lots of buttons in front of him. He wonders what they are for. He pushes some of them. Nothing happens.

'The man sits in that other seat' thinks Charlie, and he moves into the driver seat. 'Now the big black car will carry me someplace. The man puts his hands here' thinks the monkey as he stands on his hind legs and grips the black round thing with his paws. The big black car does not move. Charlie looks out the window and presses harder with his paws. The big black car sits still. 'Oh, there is another round thing', thinks Charlie, and he pushes hard on the thing in the middle of the round thing. The big black car still does not move, but it makes a terrible noise. It must be broken.

The man runs out of the house. He does not smile. He waves his arms, and he screams something. Charlie screams something back at him. The man reaches for the door handle. Charlie reaches out the window and slaps the man on the hand. The man backs away. Then the man says some loud angry words. Charlie spreads his teeth and screams something back at the man. This is his big black car now, the man must go away.

The man backs up and looks around. Then he picks up a long stick. He pushes the stick right through the window straight at Charlie's head. Charlie does not understand why the man is so mean. Charlie grabs the end of the stick and pushes it back at the man. The man pushes again, and Charlie pushes again. Two can play this game. Push—push—push—push. Finally, the man walks away. He goes to the other side of the big black car. Charlie jumps out the window and starts to go home. He does not like the mean man. He does not like the big black car. It is broken, it will not move. Charlie does not want the big black car anymore.

Known by Name

Queen Lillie and her entourage entered the church building. The Sunday morning service had already begun. It is the custom of the Royal Family to arrive late at every public gathering. That way everyone present will know that Royalty is in the house. The Queen made her way down the center aisle and seated herself on the front pew. If anyone had been seated in that row they would have risen and found seating elsewhere. Following her were two female bodyguards who took seats in row two directly behind the Queen. The male guard and the male automobile driver took seats near the rear of the sanctuary where they could witness everything going on. It is customary for someone who knows the Queen to come forward and sit with her. I had watched that happen many times. This day no one moved. I had met the queen several times, so I rose, went forward, greeted her, and sat next to the Queen.

In this country, and perhaps in others, there is a saying, "As the King goes, so goes the nation". That certainly means that as the king's family grows, so also grows the nation. If the King does something, all the men of the country are encouraged to do the same. Swaziland is a land where the King takes several wives, and all men are also urged to do so. Queen Lillie was not the first but at the time of this writing, (2006) she was one of thirteen wives.

The Prince was young when the old King died, therefore, the Queen Mother had the final say on what happened in the nation until her son took over complete rule when he had his 40th birthday. The true love of the Prince was Rose, who was his high school sweetheart. He wanted no other wife but her and promised her he would not marry another. When his schooling was finished, they married. However, the Queen Mother and the chieftains had other plans. They adhered to the custom of plural wives so the nation would grow. At that time Swaziland had the highest percentage of HIV-positive people in the world, and at the time of this writing, they still do. The death rate was exceeding the birth rate. The kingdom was dwindling. The King must have more wives so he could have more children and the nation would grow also. He was pressured. It is said that something can happen to a King who does not support the wishes of his chieftains. That would be a very scary position for a man to be in.

So, one of the chiefs gave a gift, a girl of his tribe, to be a wife of the King. Then a second chief gave Lillie to be another wife of the King. These girls were called the first two Queens. Rose, though his first wed, became Queen number three. Although he did not always do it, each year at the Reed Dance, the King was expected to choose one of the virgin girls to be a new Queen. Thousands of girls come from every village in the country, to honor the Queen Mother, and dance before the King clad in skimpy lacey garments of yarn and flowers. The citizens of Swaziland think that it is of great advantage to have a family member as a Queen. She would live in her own palace of luxury, and the family would receive favors from the Kingdom. The king lives in a palace of his own. Queen Lillie was now sharing her husband with twelve other wives, and her every move was guarded. She only saw her husband when he chose to see her.

After the service ended Queen Lillie, hugged me. She called me by my name and talked with me. Think of that—the Queen called me by name. Nothing could be of a higher honor than that except to be called by name by the King. That did not happen. He did not know me and did not care to know me.

But I know another King. A King far greater than the King of a small kingdom. It is the King of Kings. The King of the universe. Scripture tells me that He knows more than just my name. He knew me before I had a name. That is an honor that cannot be exceeded. *"Before I shaped you in the womb, I knew all about you. Before you saw the light of day, I had holy plans for you:" (Jeremiah 1:5,(The Message)*

How much closer do you really want to get:

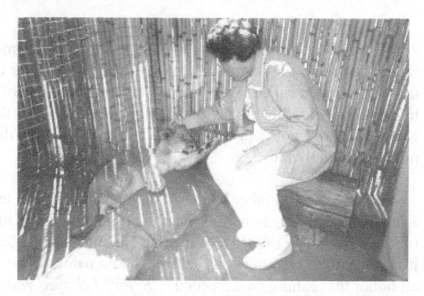

The author in the Petting Zoo, South Africa

King of the Jungle, Lion Park in South Africa

A Vacation to Remember

It was project time on our college campus. I, along with Art and Betty Littlefield, had taken advantage of the no-class week to vacation in South Africa. We had already journeyed down Highway 2 on the eastern coastline. We had experienced the opportunity to dip our toes in the warm Indian Ocean. Now we sat on the veranda of a small hotel enjoying a leisurely breakfast. A large Warbler tree grew in the swampy backyard below us.

In tropical wetlands, Warbler trees flourish. For many centuries in the past, natives living in areas where the Warbler trees grew considered them to be poisonous This was because very often people who had been near them came down with a dreaded illness. We now know that it was bites from the misquotes breeding in the swampy areas, not the trees, that gave the people malaria.

There is probably a correct name for the tree, but it is commonly known by the name Warbler because it is the nesting place for Warbler birds. These birds are very small, yellow with a touch of black, and look very much like the Canaries. Since we were vacationing during the beginning of the mating season, we had the privilege of watching the actions of the birds as they built their nests. A huge bird city was in the process of construction. The male birds were the designers and builders. The female birds were the inspectors.

The tree below us made us think of a partially decorated Christmas tree. There were dozens, perhaps hundreds of tiny baskets' hanging like Christmas balls from every branch of the tree. Each basket was about the size of a human fist, and they were all in various stages of development.

The busy little birds were darting around and about the tree, building and inspecting the nests during construction. Some buildings appeared to be perfectly rounded, some lopsided, and some in odd shapes. The male birds were working hard, gathering grasses, and weaving them into basket-like homes. His female mate was watching and approving or disapproving of the structure.

As we watched we noticed one female who was dissatisfied with her home. While her husband carefully wove the grasses into the house, she just as diligently pulled them out and tossed them aside. Finally, she found the grass that had its connection to the tree limb. As she pulled that grass out, the tiny basket home began its tumble into the swamp below. When this happened, the male had to start his building program all over again.

That poor little husband. I wondered how he felt. Did that rejection of his work hurt his male ego? Did the blatant disapproval of his mate damage their relationship? Did it lead to disharmony in that little bird family?

It makes me think about human society. Are we sometimes so ungrateful in words and deeds that it damages the serenity of our homes? Do our family and friend relationships suffer from our insisting on our own way? Our thoughts, then our words and actions come from the way we consider ourselves in a relationship with others. The wisest man of all time, Solomon, wrote the following words of advice to all of us. *"Keep thy heart with all diligence; for out of it are the issues of life". (Prov 4:23 KJV)*

Zebra in Hlane Game Reserve, Swaziland

Cultural Day Barbequed
at Local High School

Worthless?

Bobbie stood on the edge of the Dunga *(gully)*. Was that man right? Bobbie reached up and fingered the chain that hung from his neck. Was it that bad? This bright silver chain had been given to him by a friend. He really liked the gift. It reminded him of the relationship with that friend that he remembered so fondly. He removed the chain from around his neck and looked at it more closely. It had discolored. It no longer gleamed brightly. When had it turned dark? He had not noticed the blackness that had so slowly covered each link.

That fellow was so rude. He insulted Bobbie's good judgment when he asked, "Why are you wearing that worthless, dirty, black chain? It looks awful". That is no way to talk with anyone. Bobbie fingered the chain again. Maybe that person is right? This chain does not look pretty like it did when it was new. It is turning black. It actually does not look very good anymore. Maybe it is worthless.

Bobbie clutched the chain in his right hand, raised his arm, and with all his strength threw the chain into the center of the dung. He watched as it disappeared between the leaves of the thick foliage in the gully below, where it would sink forever in the mud of the cavern and be forever lost to human sight. So much for an ugly old black worthless chain…

OH! If Bobbie only knew! It is only high-grade silver that turns black! There are chemicals available that will remove all traces of tarnish.   The chain was not worthless, it was valuable! It was pure silver!

I wonder. Is human life a little bit like that silver chain? We start life so pure, so sweet, we smell so good and we are loved. As the days, months, and years went by each of us began to tarnish.   We pick up habits and activities that we know we should not. We learn to do things that we, ourselves, disapprove of. Our attitudes sometimes stink! We may be told by others that we are worthless and that we will never amount to anything.   Sometimes we believe them, and we consider that we might as well jump into the dunga and end all association with humanity.

But that is not the case! We may be tarnished even to the point of blackness, but under the dirty cover is silver! All we need is cleansing. There is a chemical strong enough to do that. The prophet said, *(Psalm 51:7) "Purge me with hyssop,* (a reference to the blood of Jesus Christ) *and I shall be clean; wash me, and I shall be whiter than snow".*   Cleansing removes the ugly blackness and causes the brilliance of the silver to shine through. Cleansing is available for the asking!

Epilogue

Thank you for traveling with me through the pages of this book. I hope you have enjoyed the journey.

As I walked through these stories I was surprised at how often I saw life lessons portrayed. Sometimes they were in the reactions of other humans or animals. Sometimes they were associated with nature. I wonder, is this the way the creator sometimes chooses to nudge me to live a life more pleasing to Him, and more enjoyable for myself and others? Did it make you examine your own life also?

For example, take another look at the High Wire story. Until I saw the problem of the monkey I never realized the lesson my own High Wire experience taught me. I am glad that I have been placed in God's gondola. If you have not, it is very easy to get there. Simply ask the pilot of the gondola to take you on board.

Again, thank you for accompanying me. If you enjoyed this experience, you might also enjoy my other books listed on Amazon. The release date of an interesting account of one of my students 'and the genocide in Central Africa is expected to be near the end of 2024

And now—" *The Lord bless thee, and keep thee: The Lord make his face shine upon thee, and be gracious unto thee: The Lord lift up his countenance upon thee, and give thee peace. (Numbers 6:25-27)*

Made in the USA
Middletown, DE
04 December 2023

43915253R00056